READ ABOUT
Castles

Tim Wood

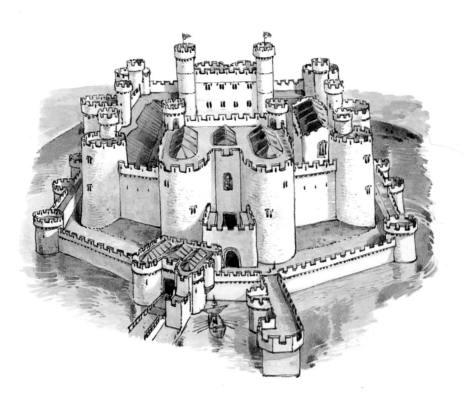

WARWICK PRESS
New York/London/Toronto/Sydney

Published in 1990 by Warwick Press,
387 Park Avenue South, New York, New York 10016.
First published in 1989 by Kingfisher Books Ltd.
Copyright © Grisewood & Dempsey Ltd. 1989.

Library of Congress Catalog Card No. 89-22553
ISBN 0-531-19071-4

Printed in Spain

Contents

If you find an unusual or difficult word in this book, check for an explanation in the glossary on pages 30 and 31.

Siege!

The siege has begun! Soldiers rush toward the castle, raise their ladders, and start to climb. Catapults shoot rocks over the walls. The castle gates shudder as an iron-tipped battering ram smashes into them. The defenders draw their bows, and arrows rain down on the attackers. The air vibrates with the noise of battle.

Today, most castles are empty ruins. As you read this book you will find out what they used to be like hundreds of years ago.

What is a Castle?

The castle was a home — but it was also a well-protected fortress where people were safe from attack. Many castles were built to defend important places such as towns, ports, and roads. Some were built by rich barons and knights who wanted to protect their lands. Castles often changed over the years as new types of defenses were added.

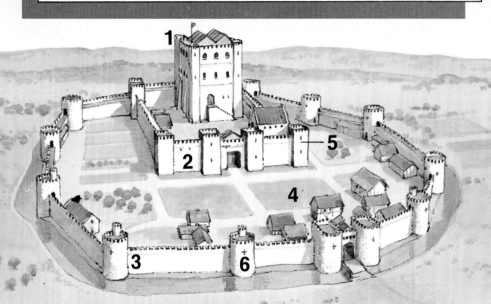

KEY TO A FORTRESS HOME

1. The keep was usually built first. It was the strongest part of the castle.
2. The inner curtain wall was often protected by towers.
3. An outer curtain wall might be added later.
4. Large yards called baileys could shelter many people.
5. Arrow slits in the wall protected the archers inside.
6. Cross-shaped arrow slits were used by crossbowmen when firing at enemies.

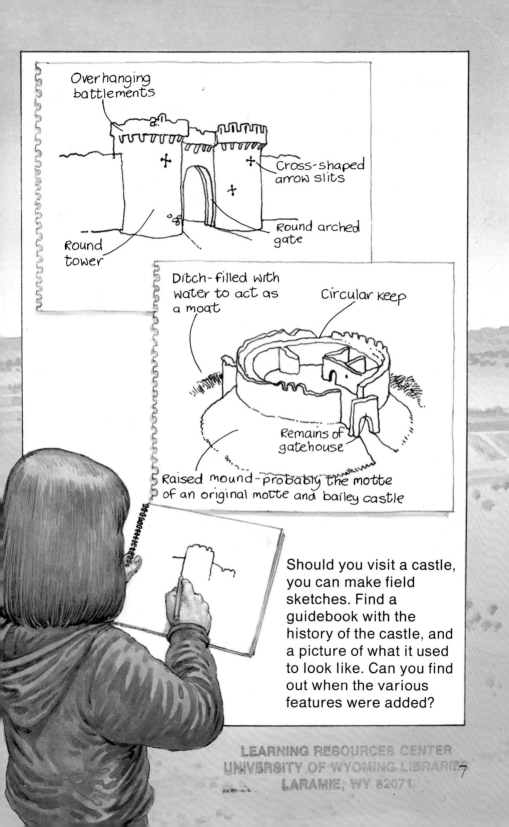

Overhanging battlements

Cross-shaped arrow slits

Round arched gate

Round tower

Ditch- filled with water to act as a moat

Circular keep

Remains of gatehouse

Raised mound-probably the motte of an original motte and bailey castle

Should you visit a castle, you can make field sketches. Find a guidebook with the history of the castle, and a picture of what it used to look like. Can you find out when the various features were added?

7

The First Castles

The first castles, called motte and bailey castles, were built about 900 years ago. The motte was a mound of earth, and the wooden tower was the strongest part of the castle. The bailey was a yard surrounded by a wooden fence, or palisade, for keeping animals.

MAKE A MOTTE AND BAILEY CASTLE

◄ Make a paste from 7 ounces flour and $\frac{1}{2}$ pint water. Tear up strips of newspaper, dip into the paste, and use to cover the outside of a bowl. Leave to dry before peeling off and trimming. Paint the motte green.

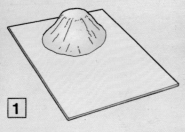

1

2

► For walls, cut drinking straws into 2-inch lengths. Place these on sticky tape, as shown.

3

▲ Make the towers and other buildings out of cut-up milk cartons. Glue straws on the outside.

▼ Make a ladder from two straws with smaller pieces glued on for rungs. For a drawbridge, cover a square of cardboard with straws.

Attach with thread.

4

9

Stone Castles

Stronger stone walls soon replaced the wooden palisades. Poorer knights, who could not afford to build castles, put up strongly built manor houses on their land. The peasants farmed the fields and paid for the knight's protection with crops and work.

Some castles were just stone towers called keeps. They had thick walls up to 100 feet high. Some had entrances high off the ground to make them harder to capture.

Concentric Castles

In about 1250, kings and nobles began to build a new type of castle. It was called a concentric castle, and it had two sets of curtain walls. If the attackers broke through the outer curtain, they still had to capture the inner one. A concentric castle often had no central keep. Instead, it had a large inner bailey with living areas built against the walls. The entrance was usually defended by a large gatehouse, or barbican.

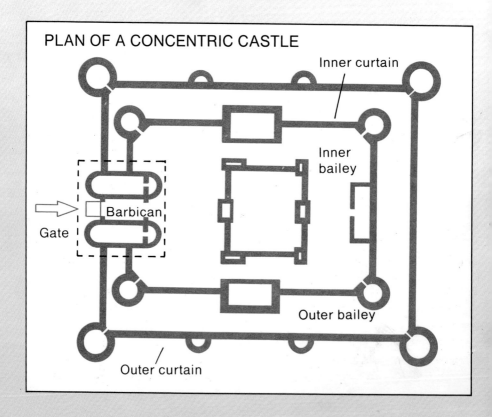

PLAN OF A CONCENTRIC CASTLE

Inner curtain

Inner bailey

Gate

Barbican

Outer bailey

Outer curtain

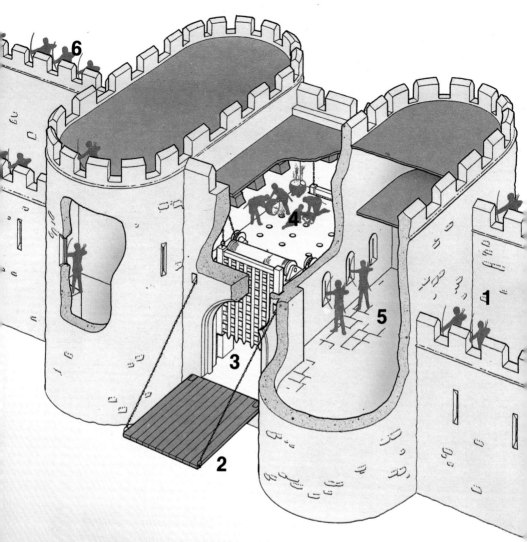

KEY TO BARBICAN

1. Archers could sweep away attackers from the gate with a storm of arrows.

2. A drawbridge was raised to block the gate.

3. A portcullis was lowered.

4. Defenders dropped rocks and boiling water or hot sand through murder holes on to the attackers who were trapped in the barbican.

5. Archers could fire at the attackers through holes in the wall of the barbican.

6. Archers on the higher, inner curtain could fire over the heads of the defenders on the lower, outer curtain.

13

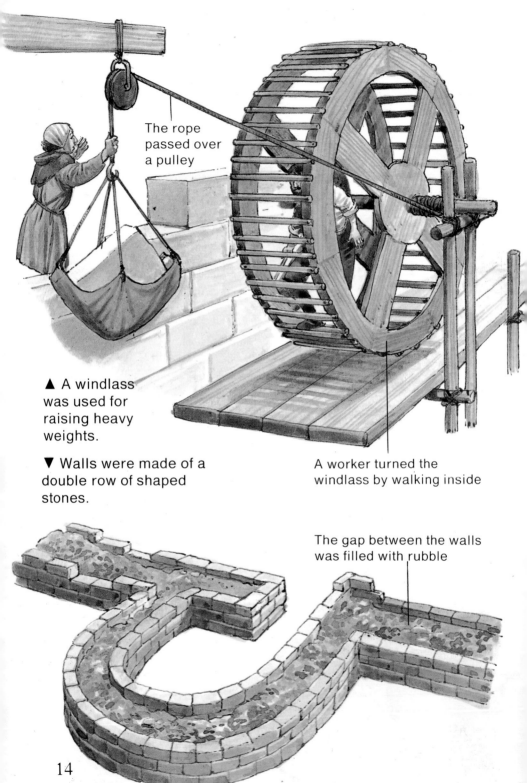

The rope passed over a pulley

▲ A windlass was used for raising heavy weights.

▼ Walls were made of a double row of shaped stones.

A worker turned the windlass by walking inside

The gap between the walls was filled with rubble

14

How a Castle was Built

A large castle could take as long as ten years to build. A skilled master mason was in charge of the work. Masons shaped the stones and carpenters cut the wood, while peasants supplied the hard labor. There were few machines, which meant that heavy work such as digging the moat was done by hand.

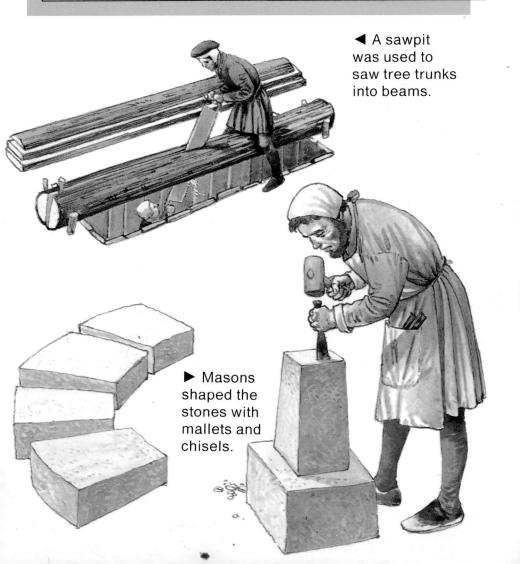

◄ A sawpit was used to saw tree trunks into beams.

► Masons shaped the stones with mallets and chisels.

Living in a Castle

The castle was just like a little town, with its own carpenters, thatchers, blacksmiths, and armorers. There were also all kinds of servants to look after the baron and

Castle keep

KEY TO CASTLE
1. Spiral staircase
2. Bedroom
3. Chapel
4. Great Hall
5. Kitchen
6. Store room — one was used as a dungeon
7. Garderobe (lavatory)
8. Stables
9. Blacksmith's workshop

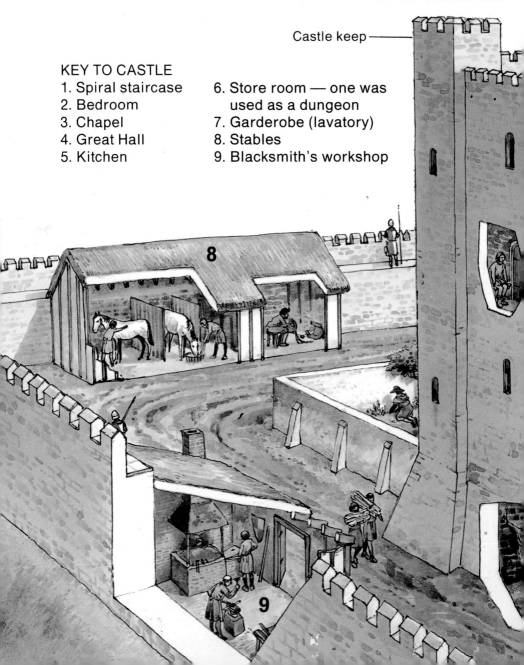

his family. Each castle would be well stocked with soldiers and supplies in case of a siege.

Look at the spiral staircase in the keep. This always wound up to the right, to make it easy for defending soldiers to use their swords against attackers.

A Banquet

Banquets were held on special occasions. The food was prepared in the large castle kitchen. Meat was roasted on a spit over an open fire, and vegetables were boiled in a cauldron.

All meals were served in the Great Hall. This was the grandest and busiest room in the castle. The lord, his lady and important guests ate at the "high table" at the end of the hall.

Kitchen fireplaces were big enough to roast a whole ox or pig!

18

The guests ate with their fingers, using big slices of bread for plates. They threw scraps and bones onto the floor.

Minstrels and jesters entertained the guests.

A Tournament

When knights were not at war, they practiced their fighting skills in tournaments. Although these were mock fights with blunt weapons, knights could still be killed or badly injured. Winners were awarded the horse and armor of the losers.

Tournaments were often held on holidays, or when important visitors were staying at the castle.

MAKE A KNIGHT'S HELMET

  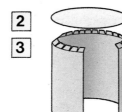 

1. Cut out a piece of card which will fit around your head, as here.

2. Cut out a circle for the top.
3. Cut and fold the tabs.

4. Tape the top of the helmet onto the tabs, as shown.

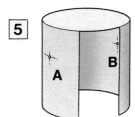 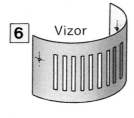 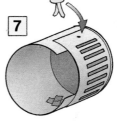

5. Mark points A and B halfway around the helmet on each side.

6. Cut a shape like this out of card. It should be deep enough to cover your face, and wide enough to fasten at A and B.

7. Fasten vizor to helmet at A and B with brass paper fasteners. Cover the inside with tape.

Roll up cut paper into a tube and fasten with tape

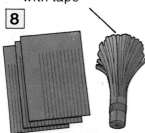

8. Make a plume from colored paper. Make a hole in the top of the helmet, push the base of the plume through and tape in place. Now paint the helmet.

21

Siege Engines

During a siege, the attackers used many different methods to weaken a castle's strength. They would stop food stores from being delivered, in the hope of starving the enemy out. At the same time, they stormed the walls with siege equipment.

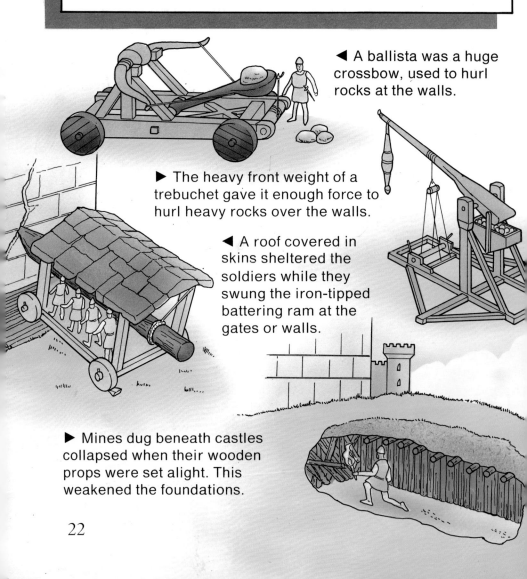

◀ A ballista was a huge crossbow, used to hurl rocks at the walls.

▶ The heavy front weight of a trebuchet gave it enough force to hurl heavy rocks over the walls.

◀ A roof covered in skins sheltered the soldiers while they swung the iron-tipped battering ram at the gates or walls.

▶ Mines dug beneath castles collapsed when their wooden props were set alight. This weakened the foundations.

MAKE YOUR OWN SIEGE CATAPULT

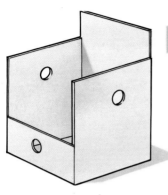

1 ◀ Cut the top off a milk carton, and cut into this shape. Make a hole in both sides and one in the back, as shown.

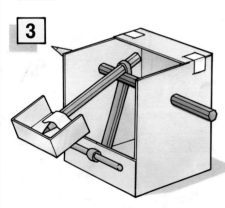

Front

▶ Thread a small rubber band through the hole in the back and hold it in place with a used match or small piece of wood. Push a pencil through the holes in the sides.

2

Back

3

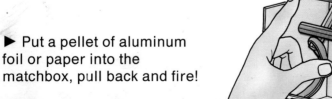

◀ Cut the tray of a matchbox in half and tape it to another pencil. Loop the rubber band over the end of the pencil as shown. Fold the front flap and tape it down.

4

▶ Put a pellet of aluminum foil or paper into the matchbox, pull back and fire!

The End of Castles

After 1450, castles slowly but steadily became less useful. The invention of gunpowder meant that cannons could be used to batter down castle walls. Only kings were rich enough to pay for the expensive guns, or for castles which could stand up to cannon fire. At the same time, as kings became more powerful, so the land became more peaceful. Nobles no longer needed to keep their own armies. They began to leave their drafty uncomfortable castles and move into large country houses.

AN EARLY CANNON
The rammer was used to pack the powder and ball into the barrel. A fuse fired the gun. The worm cleared the barrel after firing. Wedges were hit with a mallet to raise and lower the barrel.

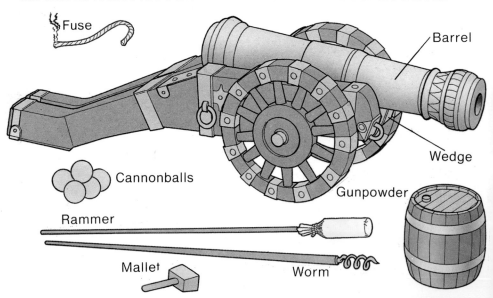

Fuse

Barrel

Cannonballs

Wedge

Gunpowder

Rammer

Mallet

Worm

Castles became important again during the English Civil War of 1642–48. Cheaper guns became available, and the defenders would return the enemy's gunfire from defenses built *outside* the castle walls. Whenever Oliver Cromwell, the Parliamentary leader, captured a Royalist castle, he blew up the walls with gunpowder after the enemy had been defeated.

Castle Ghosts

Many castles have their own ghosts. At the Tower of London, the Countess of Salisbury is said to run through the corridors, chased by her executioner. Anne Boleyn has also been seen there. Glamis Castle, one of Scotland's most haunted buildings, has a lady in gray and a ghostly carriage. And anyone who sees its "Nameless Horror" is driven mad!

Anne Boleyn

The "Nameless Horror"

The Lady in Gray

A Castle Visit

If you ever visit a castle it will probably be in ruins. But if you find the right clues, you will be able to imagine what it used to be like hundreds of years ago. As you walk around, make a plan of the castle. Mark the main features, such as the walls and towers. Then try to work out where the main living rooms were. On the opposite page are some of the main clues to look for as you go around.

To help you imagine what a castle looked like, try to find out as many details as possible about the lords and ladies who lived there, and what happened to them.

DISCOVERING RUINED CASTLES

The castle opposite is a ruin, but the picture below shows you what it looked like when it was new. The seven numbered clues below will also help you to imagine what any castle you visit used to be like hundreds of years ago.

1. Grooves in the gatehouse wall will show where the portcullis was.

2. Fireplace and holes for floor beams will show where each floor was.

3. The shape of some rooms will be shown by the remains of the foundations.

4. The remains of spiral staircases may be seen in turrets and towers.

5. Stains or lines of stones will show where buildings used to lean against the walls — such as the buildings shown in the picture below.

6. The remains of walls will show what they used to look like.

7. Holes in the wall will show where the chains of the drawbridge ran.

Glossary

Bailey
An open courtyard in a castle.

Ballista
A huge crossbow used to hurl rocks at castle walls.

Barbican
A fortified (strengthened) gatehouse.

Baron
An important nobleman who owned much land and at least one castle.

Battering ram
An iron-tipped tree trunk which was swung against castle walls and gates to batter them down.

Catapult
A siege machine used for hurling rocks at castle walls.

Cauldron
An iron cooking pot. It hung on an iron chain over an open fire.

Concentric castle
A castle with two or more rings of walls, one inside the other. The inner walls were higher than the outer ones.

Curtain
The wall of a castle.

Drawbridge
A wooden bridge into a castle which could be swung up to block the entrance.

Foundations
The stone base of the walls of a building.

Keep
The massive central tower of a castle.

Mason
A skilled craftsman who cut and shaped stone.

Mine
A tunnel dug under castle walls by the attackers. The roof was propped up with wood which was finally set on fire. The tunnel then collapsed, causing the walls to crack and fall.

Minstrel
A musician.

Motte
An artificial mound on which an early castle was built. Later castles were too heavy for mottes and so they were put up on firm, level ground.

Palisade
A wooden wall.

Parliamentarians
Supporters of the Parliament during the English Civil War.

Portcullis
A castle gate which was pierced with holes so that when it was lowered the defenders could fire arrows through it.

Rammer
A wooden tool which was used to ram the powder, wad, and cannonball tightly into the barrel of a cannon.

Royalists
Supporters of King Charles I during the English Civil War.

Siege
An attack on a castle.

Tournament
A contest between knights who fought a series of mock battles called jousts.

Trebuchet
A type of catapult. Its power was provided by a large weight in the front.

Vizor
The hinged flap on the front of a helmet which protected the knight's face. It was pierced with eye holes to let the knight see where he was going.

Wad
A pad rammed into the muzzle of a cannon to make an airtight seal in the barrel. This made the gunpowder explode with more force.

Wedge
A piece of wood placed under the barrel of a cannon. Hitting it inward with a malle raised the barrel.

Windlass
A machine for lifting heavy weights. It worked by levers or a treadmill winding up a rope on an axle.

Index

archers 6, 13
armor 20
armorer 16
arrow slit 6, 7
arrows 4, 13, 31

bailey 6, 8, 12, 30
ballista 22, 30
barbican 12, 13, 30
baron 6, 16, 30
battering ram 4, 22, 30
blacksmith 16

cannons 24, 31
carpenters 15, 16
catapult 4, 23, 30, 31
cauldron 18, 30
Civil War 25, 31
concentric castle 12, 30
Cromwell, Oliver 25
curtain 6, 12, 13, 30

defenses 6, 25
drawbridge 9, 13, 29, 30
dungeon 16, 27

foundation 22, 29, 30

gate 4, 7, 12, 13, 22, 30, 31
gatehouse 7, 12, 29, 30
ghosts 26, 27
Glamis Castle 26
Great Hall 16, 18

gunpowder 24, 25, 31

jesters 19

keep 6, 10, 12, 16, 17, 30
kitchen 16, 18
kitchen garden 16

ladders 4, 9

masons 15, 30
mines 22, 30
minstrel 19, 31
moat 7, 15
motte and bailey castle 7, 8
murder holes 13

palisade 8, 10, 31
peasants 10, 15
portcullis 13, 29, 31

sawpit 15
siege 4, 17, 22, 30, 31
siege towers 22
soldiers 4, 17, 22

tournament 20, 31
tower 6, 9, 28, 29, 30
Tower of London 26
trebuchet 22, 31

walls 4, 6, 8, 10, 12, 14, 22, 24, 25, 28, 29, 30, 31
wedge 24, 31
windlass 14, 31

32

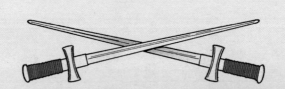